FOLGER McKINSEY ELEMENTARY SCHOOL

The World of Composers

Handel

Greta Cencetti

PETER BEDRICK BOOKS

McGraw-Hill
Children's Publishing
A Division of The **McGraw·Hill** Companies

This edition published in the United States in 2002 by
Peter Bedrick Books, an imprint of
McGraw-Hill Children's Publishing,
A Division of The McGraw-Hill Companies
8787 Orion Place
Columbus, Ohio 43240

www.MHkids.com

ISBN 1-58845-470-3

Library of Congress Cataloging-in-Publication Data

Cencetti, Greta.
Handel / Greta Cencetti.
p. cm. -- (The world of composers)
Summary: An introduction to the life and music
of the eighteenth-century German composer.
ISBN 1-58845-470-3
1. Handel, George Frederick, 1685-1759. [1. Handel, George Frederick,
1685-1759. 2. Composers.] I. Title. II. Series.

ML3930.H25 C46 2002
780'.92--dc21
[B]
2001052904

10 9 8 7 6 5 4 3 2 1 CHRT 06 05 04 03 02

Printed in China.

The World of Composers

Handel

Greta Cencetti

PETER BEDRICK BOOKS

Contents

Hallẽ

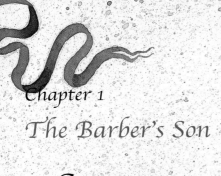

Chapter 1

The Barber's Son

Georg Friederich Handel was born on February 23, 1685, in the small German town of Halle. His parents were Dorothea and Georg Handel. Handel used the name *Georg Friederich* in later life in Germany, and the English version, *George Frederick*, after he moved to England.

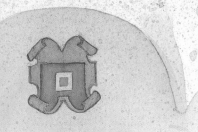

Handel's father was a barber and surgeon. His mother was a music lover. When she set up a household with Georg Handel, she brought along her beloved musical instruments. She kept them in a large room in the Handel home.

Young George was fascinated by the instruments in this room. His mother noticed his interest and began teaching him scales and basic musical concepts.

Chapter 2
A Visit With the Duke

One day, Handel's father took him to the home of the Duke of Saxe-Weissenfels. Young George began to wander around the large room while his father cut the Duke's hair. There, he discovered a harpsichord, a musical instrument that looks like a small version of today's piano. George climbed onto the music stool and placed his small hands on the keys. Soon, he was playing the music his mother had taught him.

The Duke was surprised when he heard the music. He was even more surprised when he realized that it was the little boy who was playing. The Duke told Handel's father that the child should develop his talent.

Handel's father thanked the Duke, but told him that he wanted George to study law rather than music. The Duke understood, but did not agree. He offered to pay for young Handel's education if the boy studied music instead of law.

Chapter 3
The Young Musician

*H*andel's father could not refuse the generosity of the Duke. He arranged for his nine-year-old son to take music lessons from Friedrich Zachow, who was a well-known organist.

Zachow took a strong interest in young Handel and taught him how to play the organ, violin, oboe, and harpsichord. Handel later became his teacher's assistant at the church where Zachow was organist. Zachow had a close association with him until Handel later left Halle for Hamburg.

Handel's father passed away while Handel was still studying music. To honor his father's wishes, he decided to study law at the University of Halle. After he graduated, though, he focused completely on music.

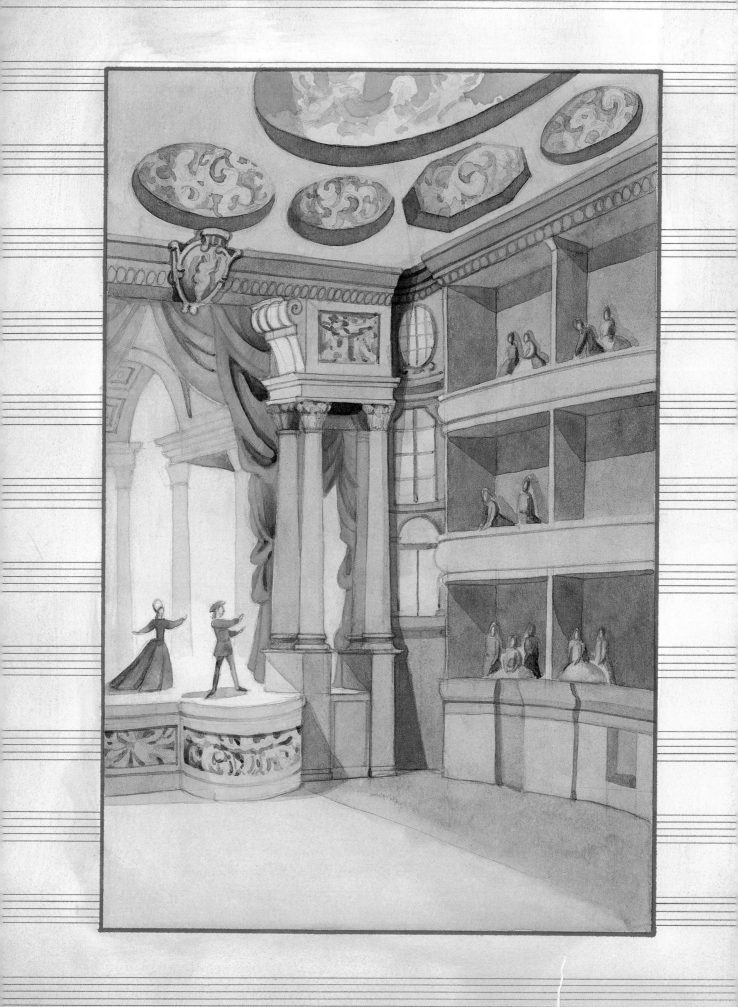

Handel soon found the city of Halle offered few opportunities for his career. He decided that there would be more opportunities in the city of Hamburg, an important musical center in Germany. Handel took a position playing the violin in an opera orchestra there, and before long he was composing his own operas.

Chapter 4
The Day of the Duel

*I*n Hamburg, Handel met a composer named Johann Mattheson, who was four years older than he was. Although Mattheson was not easy to get along with, Handel became his friend. Though friends, the two had a serious argument about music that led to a duel.

The duel took place on the square in front of the opera house where one of Handel's operas was being performed. The duel attracted a lot of attention, but neither man was hurt during the fight. Mattheson's sword hit a large button on Handel's coat, and Mattheson was saved by a thick musical score he had in his pocket. Later, they were able to rebuild their friendship.

One day, Handel and Mattheson learned that a new organist was needed in a nearby city named Lübeck. They both left right away to try out for the job.

In Lübeck, there was an unwritten rule. It was understood that the person who took over the position of organist would marry the daughter of Dietrich Buxtehude, the present organist. Neither Handel nor Mattheson were interested in marriage, so they both returned to Hamburg.

Chapter 5
Fame and Fortune in Italy

By this time, Handel had written a number of successful operas and was becoming wealthy. His newfound wealth gave him the opportunity to travel to Italy.

Italy was an important country for music at that time. Many great composers lived there, and Handel was eager to learn from them. In 1706, at the age of 21, he began his journey to Italy, visiting Venice, then Florence, Rome, and Naples.

During his travels in Italy, Handel met a number of important contemporary composers, including Arcangelo Corelli and Alessandro Scarlatti.

Handel worked on a number of new operas. Most of them were well received. His admirers found that his music expressed joy and a celebration of life.

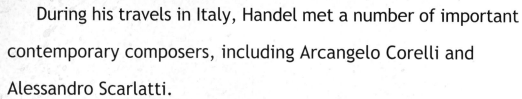

Handel met many other powerful people in Italy, including Cardinal Vincenzo Grimani, the ruler of Naples. Grimani was an important politician and a writer. Soon, he became one of Handel's biggest fans. Grimani suggested that he and Handel write an opera together. He would write the lyrics and Handel would write the music. Together they created the opera *Agrippina*.

Agrippina is a fictional story set in Rome that is based on several historical characters and real events which occurred around 50 A.D. *Agrippina* tells the tale of the emperor Claudius' wife, Agrippina, and her plot to make sure that her son, Nero, becomes the next emperor. The opera was very popular, and 27 performances followed.

In 1710, Handel went to Hanover, Germany, basking in his success. There, he was appointed "Kappellmeister" (choirmaster) to the Elector, who later became King George I of England. Soon after, though, Handel accepted an invitation to move to London.

Chapter 6
Life in London

*T*he thought of living in London was so interesting to Handel that he did not wait to get permission from the Elector before leaving Hanover. He arrived in London in November of 1710 at the age of 25.

London was an exciting city. There were many artistic events, and music was everywhere. Handel became well-known in the city. Even Queen Anne expressed her appreciation of his music by awarding him a royal pension (salary) in 1713.

The popular composer soon made new friends, including a man named Richard Boyle, the Earl of Burlington. Both the Earl and his mother admired Handel's music.

George I, who had been Elector of Hanover, took over the throne when Queen Anne died. The King was still angry with Handel for leaving his job as choirmaster in Hanover without his permission. Richard Boyle let Handel hide in his home to escape the anger of the King.

George I did not punish Handel after all, but allowed him to continue composing. During this time, Handel wrote one of his most famous works, *Water Music*.

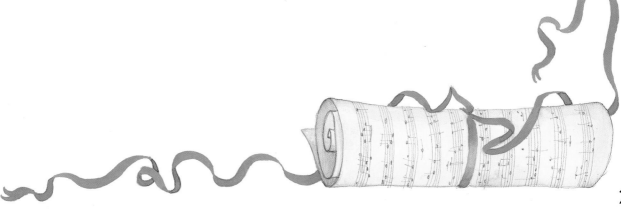

Water Music, an orchestral piece, was first performed in 1717 as King George I and his followers traveled down the Thames River, a river that flows through London. The event was staged to make the King more visible to his subjects as he headed down the river to Hampton Court Palace. Music was heard everywhere and fireworks lit up the sky.

Handel became very successful, and in 1719 he became the dean of the Royal Academy of Music.

In the years that followed, aside from visiting his mother in Halle, Handel spent most of his time composing. He had been given the task of composing operas for the new opera house in London, so he also traveled around, in search of new singers.

In 1733, a group of people became jealous of Handel's success. They began to write articles accusing Handel of being snobbish and bossy. They soon formed a new opera company, Opera of the Nobility, that was supported by the Prince of Wales. Most of Handel's singers left him for the new company. Although the King and Queen of England still favored Handel and attended his operas, their son's encouragement of his enemies hurt Handel. Almost no one came to his performances.

Chapter 7
Success of *Messiah*

Handel's health began to decline. One day during a rehearsal, a doctor had to be called in to take care of Handel's leg and eye ailments.

The composer was advised to rest, but because he had always been such an active person, he did not follow this advice. In fact, he worked harder, creating new works, many of which had religious themes.

Disappointed by his experience with the British royal family, Handel decided to move to Ireland in 1741. He settled in Dublin, the capital of Ireland. There, surrounded by beautiful scenery, he completed another famous work, the *Messiah*.

The *Messiah* received great acclaim, and Handel's audiences grew. To make extra space in the theater so that more people could attend, the organizer of the *Messiah* made special rules. Ladies were asked not to wear the bulky dresses that were in style at the time to the theater. The men were asked not to bring swords.

Not long after these performances, Handel returned to England. The *Messiah* was such a success when it was performed in London, that the new king, George II, attended more than one show. It is said that he stood throughout an entire performance of this great work to show his respect for Handel. Even today, audiences show this same respect by standing throughout the "Hallelujah Chorus," the *Messiah's* most famous piece.

Chapter 8
Perseverance

Handel continued to suffer from ill health. His eyesight was weakening, and eventually he became blind. When he performed, he had to be placed on the stool in front of the organ.

His last work was an *oratorio*, a musical piece that features singing. This oratorio was entitled *Jephtha*, and Handel finished it in 1757. In the notes that he attached to this famous work he wrote, in German, that the sight in his left eye had become so poor that he could not continue. He worked at a slower pace than usual, but was finally able to complete the piece.

allegro ma non troppo

Chapter 9

The Man and the Monument

George Frederick Handel died on April 14, 1759. After Handel was buried in Westminster Abbey, one of London's most famous churches, a monument was built in his honor. His boundless energy and superb musical skills made him one of the most important composers and musicians of the Baroque period.

Introduction to Opera

Opera is just one of the many musical forms at which Handel excelled. This expressive art form combines singing, drama, orchestral music, and sometimes dance, in a theater setting. Most operas include elaborate scenery and costumes. There are two basic parts to an opera: the text, or *libretto,* and the music, or *score.*

Opera has its roots in ancient Greek tragedies, which were performed along with music. One of the original operas that resembles those we see today was performed in the late 1500s, in Florence, Italy. This opera was based on the legend of the gods Daphne and Apollo.

The first public opera house opened in 1637 in Venice, Italy. It was called the Teatro S. Cassiano. The operas that were performed there were lighthearted and melodic, and appealed to a wide range of people. The operas performed in Venice began to focus on a vocal soloist. Italy has always played a key role in the development of opera, but today opera can be heard worldwide.